Wounds to Words

AF624484

Tina Carey

BookLeaf Publishing

Presentation by *BookLeaf Publishing*

Web: www.bookleafpub.com

E-mail: info@bookleafpub.com

ISBN: 978-93-95890-21-2

First edition 2022

To Gary and Justin, who didn't make it out alive, and to me, because I did.

ACKNOWLEDGEMENT

I would like to thank the Muse Writers Center in Norfolk, Virginia, and my teachers for creating a pathway for me to reveal my authentic self. To my daughters, Mariah and Kayla, for loving me still.

a love story

she

had a decent heart
until it was stomped out and torn apart
by every lover that fed and fled.

she
prays with antique love beads
counting and rubbing between
blistered hands and crimson-stained teeth.

she

finds compassion under the leaves of the
california pepper tree, believing the ooze
from the pinkish fruit will be the
glue
that puts her back together.

she writes

between soiled ivory walls that clench secrets.
            sits in her tired-out leathery-armed chair
and waits for the perfect phrase to rupture in her
mind.
            her boney toes scratch at the cracked
wooden
floor,
digging for pain. for inspiration. for something
more-
than just
time
that leaks down the slit hourglass.
nothing lives here; even the flowers don't
move
 like her pen does
yet,
she finds a way to write through it all.
through anything
                                                            She
Writes

the wooden box

a guardian,
a tiny tomb,
protecting secrets untold.

a sunken tree of life
stains the surface,

leaves spread out
edge to edge like fragile
lungs.

clutching mother of pearl urn's
with tiny bone, salt, and minerals
locked inside.

in november i pick
up the wooden box
gently,
like a sleeping baby.

I let out a roar of
a wounded animal
a human's noiseless cry
the sounds of every mothers loss
the sonance of love that never dies.

Journey of a Tattoo

The rain flicks on the window like a knock at the door daring me to wake.

It's been 5 years and I'm still swaying between living and dying, unwilling to go in either direction. Grief shatters me in a room with all my favorite things.
yet,
nothing is tangible in this color-blind space.

I answer the door and head out into the world to make sense of this ache that has devoured every inch of my being.

I arrive; (Greg's Tattoos)

A man stands outside, a haze of smoke twists around him. With each step, the warm and woody smell of the freshly lit clove cigarette embraces me.

A red skull tattoo covers his face, with perfectly shaped black horns resting on his forehead. His old grey eyes saw the hurt in me, and he welcomed me inside.

Can I help you?

Yes, I need a tattoo. Can I have a piece of paper, please?

He bent down, shuffled through a clanky junk drawer, and handed me a frayed notepad and a half-sharpened pencil.

I drew blindly and handed him my grief.

It's beautiful, he said. What does it mean?

Without hesitation, shame or guilt, I say—

My brother Gary overdosed on heroin and died. He used to blow dandelions in my face when we were little, and my brother Justin killed himself 5 days later. He's free now.

I exhaled

We connected one human to another, and a purpose filled the room as he inked my grief.

The stem of the dandelion flows up my wrist as long as love, while spores dance around my hand as the letters f r e e spreads its wings down my arm. And blood splits my grief into something I can hold on to.

Glue

I'm a lost soul
glued
to immobile shadow.
Eyes always closed,
if I open them
trepidation
slides in,
the smell of red roses
splashed with blood,
it's enough to lose
my
fading wit.
I'll never move on,
its stays with me
like skin
to bone.

Toxic Bloom

You leave behind a hue
a toxic bloom;
make me want to know more about you,
your essence intoxicates me,
I want to see all your deformities,
your aches,
learn all your mistakes.
I want to be everything
you never knew.
I want to save you.

Tattoo

There's an emptiness
inside me
That I will never get back
A place in time
that I can't rewind.
It happened when I was barely nine,
your massive hands on my tiny body
It's a blemish
I can't scrub off.
So again I plea,
Let go of me.
You're like a
ghastly tattoo,
I'll never
get
rid of you.

48

fine lines and wrinkles haven't hit me yet but my
knees hurt and my toes pop every time i move in
any direction especially when I try to twist my
ass or curl my hair my hands crack from battle
wounds or maybe it's the old age bangin on the
door trying to wake up my 30 year old mind
which by the way was the best years of my life
oh how I miss that sudden wisdom that
connected my brain to my body that appeared at
the ocean when i realized I couldn't swim or
fuckin breathe from all the smokin i had done in
my youth that youth I still have that never sleeps
and drinks and listens to pink floyd when I'm sad
and tired

        from time

yeah

  time

ill be 48 in october

1st love

You procrastined your cruelty
until our last names matched and
my heart softened to safety.

Blackberries

In the delivery room. I
landed on the smell of my mother
even then we couldn't find each
other.

she only woke from her dead emotions
for me in june

when we searched for ripe blackberries.
she

glowed at the site of the blackish fruit.
she
awed at the perfectly shaped bush.
she

kneeled as nature's breath helped drop her
blessing.
she

tenderly plucked and cradled each one in her
dainty hand and

placed the overflow in the tiny folds of mine.
be careful
                she said.
don't hold them too tight
                she said.

the juice—
stains

if only I had never washed my hands.   at least

at least

we would have that.

You and Me

How did it come to this?
          you and me

Passing each other like freight trains moving
full speed and headed towards nothing.

We gave into love in the beginning and
now—
          and now—

We are swindling time, fighting
to the death for nickels and dimes.

We haven't touched in years yet
the desire still looms thick, like
a smoke-filled room
smeared with excuses.

Maybe it's the friends before lovers that
keeps us tied to one another, making
it impossible to transition
from a broke up marriage and
a life we tried to make with
good intentions.

Dear Lilies

I’ve always been
attracted to you,
a treat to the eyes,
vibrant and complex
only flourishing in dim light
and darkness.

The only thing that stimulates
your growth is coldness.
Like me,

We tire in the winter.
Leaves slowing dancing off
our skin,
only to come back glorious and full
when a new season begins.

Grief Knot

Grief knot

A coil of pain,
A twirl of despair.

Crossed and twisted
to bring immense pain.

After being worn for some time,
it starts to unravel.

Revealing pieces of happiness,
loosened smiles,
drops of laughter
intertwined with moments of love.

Snatch those threads,
and put them up for later.

When they transpire, the sorrow
It seems to glisten a bit.

Those are the days we need to remember.

In a world

in a world where white lies are truths
that paved the way for the government to be in
charge of our wombs/bringing back coat hangers
and back-alley delivery rooms next to trash bins
as secret tombs.

perhaps this will bring color back to their
tongues
when they see blood in the streets /from the girl
that didn't want to have her father's son.

Home

Take me to this place
you say is breezeless,
where the shadows stand still,
and the brightness is at the tips
of our toes
and the darkness smells like rainbows.

Take me to this place you say
the waves crinkle and
and never splash, where you become ageless
never knowing how
much time has passed.

Take me to this place you say
people fall in love without saying a word,
where the sunshine is vibrantly heard.

Take me to this place you and I will only know.

The Violinist

I followed the sound
that pulled me near

It's coming from the boardwalk
notes spiraling
with the ocean air

I stop—

To see a man's chin
seated on the permanent crack
in his violin.

His bow is moving
passive and powerful,
clothes frayed,
from days worn

I place money in his empty bowl.

With a glance—
I said,
I have one plea

Can you play a love song

for me
with a simple nod,
he rose from his knees

The string lit up
and he let them guide
the way.

I closed my eyes,
I floated like a wounded bird
exploring for land

Inhaling sounds
feeling the notes
with my hands

His strings begin to snap
and his hands began to bleed

I hear the drips,
as I fell to my knees

With no string left
and nothing left to break

I rise up

I thanked the stranger
for reminding me

that I am not a
mistake.

Ebony Moon

sullen moon
plays with me as I float on the coral sea

purposely hiding the
beauty underneath

the water is emotional
and warm

from the salty tears
left from the midnight
storm

my body
is bare
my spirit
roams free

as the leftover
bits of
my ebony moon

gently heal my
wounds

and whispers

I SEE YOU

The Old Guitar

pouts of madness nudge
my thumb closer to her stings.

Twenty years,

I've been playing the same melody.
My fingers have become weathered,
bloodied and dry.

I play for my devotion,
I play for someone to fall in love
with her like I am

She begs for my compassion and touch
same things humans do.

I’m drained,
from carrying around her song.

If only someone would listen, truly listen
they would finally remember what love is.

I'm dying not from age,
I'm dying from being unheard.

-pression

We walk side by side on the same streets,
molasses under our feet.
Snatching up joy like pickpocketing thieves
living off pharmaceutical candies.

Breathing in dead air that embraces our sad
tongues. Grabbing life even though it's like
trying to hold water with a closed fist.

Eventually, the mask shatters, and the truth will
reveal,

The parasite that trespasses our brains
          Slithers down our eyes
                    Steals our souls
                              Turns our limbs
into stone.

This is me
This is us

hiding from what society chooses not to see.

Like the DE
That comes before -pression.

When it becomes too loud,

the shriek from collapsed lung reaches

for the tallest building
a gun
or a knife
and it will take our lives.

I'm turning the hand before the outcome.

We.
Me.

Will keep swimming through pools filled with
honey
move even if it's up hill walking through drying
concrete to snatch joy next to you
on the street.

Self Love

It's a powerful feeling and internally freeing,
reaching deep inside your soul to find
self-love.
You will leave many behind,
and start to decline to share your space with
people who don't
share the same state
of mind.

Reaching for higher love is never worthless
it should be your purpose,
even
if you are the only one
takes notice.

The moment you realize you're enough
nothing else will matter.
You will be ready for
new chapters
and even new disasters.

Spores

a dandelion: the fragile spores
slowly separating and blowing away,
sway with the wind to places unknown.

This weed—
thriving in a concrete crack.

Discovering along the way
that for a seed to grow
it must come entirely undone
the shell bursts, its insides leak out,
destructive reconstruction,

to bloom,
be split apart
blown away
and eventually
rise again.

www.ingramcontent.com/pod-product-compliance
Lightning Source LLC
Chambersburg PA
CBHW051753130826
49812CB00033B/1132
9789395890212